Yvonne Andersen Poems

TABITHA MOSS

authorHOUSE®

AuthorHouse™
1663 Liberty Drive
Bloomington, IN 47403
www.authorhouse.com
Phone: 1 (800) 839-8640

Published by AuthorHouse 01/31/2018

ISBN: 978-1-5462-2445-7 (sc)
ISBN: 978-1-5462-2444-0 (e)

In loving memory of

Yvonne Engle

Survived by her spouse Ernest Engle, 4 siblings - Mark Gould, Barbara Gould, Thomas Gould, and Judy Gould. 4 Children - Heidi Andersen, Tabitha Moss, Bryon Andersen, and Keith Andersen , Their Spouses and 12 grandchildren.

Contents

My Friend

Written, September 10th, 1975

I have a friend
he is the best.

There's not another like
him in the whole U.S.

When he comes to my house
He's not just a quest.

When I see that he's tired,
I ask him to rest.

This friend of mine
Shall never be a pest.

I will Always

Written, December 12, 1989

I will always love you
no-matter what you do.

I will always love you
I swear to you this is true.

I will always love you
even when i'm blue

I will always love you
there will never be anyone new.

I will always love you
I hope you feel this way to.

Dear Lord

Written, January 25th, 1972

Oh dear lord,
hear my plea,
save me from insanity.

Lead me down the path to go,
teach me how to mend and sew.

Keep my man wise and clean,
keep him nice, yet not mean.

Keep him loyal, keep him safe,
teach us to live with the other race.

Guide him with your hand so pure,
he will follow I am sure.

Walk with him and talk with him,
and keep the light from going dim.

So dear Lord
hear our plea,
watch over him and me,
and keep us in the heart of thee.

A Lass

Written March 9th, 1972

I have a lass
she's in my class.

She loves to harass,
and play the brass.

She's got a glass,
and likes to sass.

She's full of gas
but she goes to mass.

Star's

Written, May 5th, 1972

Here are the star's,
all shining with glee.

There is one twinkling,
by it's light you can see.

The flowers do sleep,
for so are the bee's.

The tree's stand still,
like the silence of the sea's.

The house is all silent,
So good-night from me.

My Son

Written, January 14th, 1973

I have a son
his chores are done.

He likes the drink rum,
and shoot his gun.

He'll eat his bun's
then life a ton.

He'll be the one,
cause he's my son.

Our House

Witten, January 15th, 1973

Our house isn't to big,
we won't live like a pig.

Our house isn't to small,
there's room for all.

Our house me be a mess,
but not for guest's.

Our house may be clean,
but we're not at all mean.

Our house isn't so fancy,
that our friends can't see.

Our house isn't so dull,
for it is not yet full.

That is the story
of our little house.

The Moon

Written, April 12th, 1973

The moon is so pretty,
it has a gray light.

It shines all over
it's a wonderful sight.

When you sit under it,
it becomes light soon.

Then the beauty is gone,
but not for long.

Then away goes the sun
for its work is all done.

For here come the moon
and the shining stars.

Well good-night it
will be light soon.

Tabitha Moss

Feet

Written, April 19th, 1973

If you didn't have feet
you couldn't stand.

If you care for them
they will be grand.

If you sit in the sun
you will tan.

If your feet are strong
You can walk in the sand.

If your feet are neat
they'll be the best in the land

A Day With The Sun

Written, October 15th, 1973

As i sit in the yard
with the sun so high,

all I can hear is the
birds in the sky.

The neighbors dog
doesn't make a peep.

The little cat is
fast asleep.

As I lay in the grass
which is cool today,

I can hear the song
of a beautiful blue jay.

I can feel the sun's rays
beating down on my back,

Tabitha Moss

When I realize I am
on top of a track.

The sun is going down
And it's getting chilly,

The days at an end
todays been a dilly.

Lord

Written, November 20th, 1973

Oh lord,
hear my plea.
Change the thing's,
that shouldn't be.

Change the hate into love.
Change the hawk to a dove.

But most of all,
change the children,
from up above,
help the ones,
who can not love.

Change the suffering,
and insanity for the ones,
who can not see.

Oh my lord,
hear my plea,
I will love the
young ones of thee.

Red

Written, February 14th, 1974

I know a girl
her name is Red.

I know a man
his name is Ned.

She was no good
so they all said.

One day she ran off
with a man named Ted.

Three months later
they had to wed.

Know she's dead
from a bump on the head.

Tick-Tock

Written, February 28th, 1974

Tick-tock
Tick-tock
It's that time of gay.

Tick-tock
Tick-tock
It's time to work then play.

Tick-tock
Tick-tock
It's time to eat and pray.

Tick-tock
Tick-tock
It's the end of the day.

The World

Written, June 6th, 1974

Planes in the sky
cars zooming by,

what could be happening
to this world of you and I.

Pollution we have
and love none at all.

We're fighting a war
Peace shall be no more.

You love your neighbor
So you slam your door.

Cruelty to children
but animals no more.

You poison your lover
and murder your friends.

But for me in this world
this is the living end!

Pop

Written, July 10th, 1974

I have a Pop
he has a crop.

He uses a mop
and he eats slop.

He plays with a top,
that he likes to hop.

His crop's a flop,
now he has to stop.

People

Written, July 19th, 1974

There are many kinds of
People in this world, but
None of them are the same.

Some are small,
some are tall.

Some are skinny,
some are fat.

Some wear glasses,
some wear contacts.

Some have long hair,
some have short.

But out of all that
that isn't what makes a person.

It's what's inside their
hearts and heads that counts.

Nat

Written, August 15th, 1974

I have a cat
his name is Nat.

He chases the rat
and a big black bat.

My cat is fat,
he likes a pat.

He mewed as he sat,
And that's that.

The Sky

Written, September 18ᵗʰ, 1974

The sky is so clear
not a cloud in sight.

All I can see is a
bird in flight.

I can see the moon
on this month of May.

The breeze is a kickin
on this perfect day.

The sky is so blue
Not a gray or white spot.

Now I can see a dove
flying very high above.

Now I can tell that I
am deeply in love.

With the sun and the moon
and the stars so high and
most of all the beautiful
sky.

Ring-A-Ling

Written, December 10th, 1974

Ring-a-ling, ring-a-ling,
I know a little ding-a-ling.

Ring-a-ling, ring-a-ling,
I feel a little tickling.

Ring-a-ling, ring-a-ling,
I see a policeman signaling.

Ring-a-ling, ring-a-ling,
now my head's a tingaling.

Tabitha Moss

Fred

Written, December 18th, 1974

Fred was his name
sex was his game.

Till one night when he came.
I wasn't at all the same.

He said it was a frame
That I was to blame.

They said who that dame
It's surly a shame,

that you turn the blame
on this helpless dame.

Our Baby

Written, December 21st, 1974

Now that I carry
this child of our's.

There is no need
for candy and flowers,

When the baby want's to kick
I pray it'll never be sick.

When the doctor listen's
To my belly,

It always turns
my heart to jelly.

But when I have this
child or our's,

You can give her
the candy and flower's.

Tabitha Moss

Me

Written, January 1st, 1975

I am a woman
not much to see.

I am a person
just like you.

I can live
just like you do.

I have pigeon's
that like to coo.

I have a cow
that like's to mow.

I have a teddy bear
called little bear pooh.

I have so many animal's
It's just like a zoo.

Lue

Written, January 14th, 1975

His name is Lue
his gal was Sue.

He cook's stew
for a large crew.

Then he met Hue
which he slew.

They found his shoe
not Lue will brew.

Tell me Lue
did you do it for Sue.

Kid's

Written, January 21st, 1975

Kid's are funny in
their own little way.
They go outside,
they love to play.
When they come inside,
they have a lot to say,
kid's like to run,
they're so happy and gay.
When they go to bed,
they will always pray.

The Boat

Written, January 26th 1975

We went on a boat,
it was such fun.

We took our coat for
when there wasn't a sun.

We got in a moat,
the boat weighed a ton.

The boat wouldn't float,
now my stories all done.

The Bar

Written, February 10th, 1975

You go to work,
in your big car.

You never come home
you go to the bar.

Your with your friend's
I don't know who they are.

You're getting to loose
You're going to far.

Why Me

Written February 11ᵗʰ, 1975

Why did it happen
why did I have to see?

Why do I love you
why did it happen to me?

Why did I look
what kind of woman is she?

Why did I beg
this truly can't be?

You started to laugh
then said to me;

Get out of my life,
I want to be free.

The Crash

Written, March 7th, 1975

One horrible night
I saw a flash.

I went outside
there had been a crash.

Well she died fast
he got a deep gash.

Now he's alright
except for whiplash.

My Fish

Written, March 19th, 1975

My fish are quit
they swim all day.

They are funny in
their own little way.

My fish aren't sad
they're happy and gay.

My fish live in a tank
and that's where they stay.

Brad

Written, March 21ˢᵗ, 1975

I know a lad
His name is brad.

He like's to catch chad,
to give to his dad.

He was always glad,
Never was he sad.

He was never bad
nor was he cad.

He never got mad
he was a good lad.

Pansy's

Written, April 20ᵗʰ, 1975

Pansy's so pretty,
bright purple, yellow and red.

They look so beautiful
in my big flower bed.

Four petal's to each
so that's what they said.

So close to the ground
but they do not spread.

For pansy's next year
i'll keep the seeds in my shed.

Tabitha Moss

Bug In The Rug

Written, April 23rd, 1975

There was a bug,
who lived in a rug.

He needed a drug,
to drink from his mug.

He grabbed a jug,
and gave a big tug.

He gave it a hug,
and then went glug, glug.

And that is the story
of the bug in the rug.

He

Written, May 10th, 1975

He made a bet,
now he's in debt.

He has a pet,
now at the vet.

He was put on a jet,
now he will fret.

He had something to get
which he hadn't got yet.

He put on a net
now he's all set.

Tabitha Moss

Oh, Lord

Written, May 18th, 1975

Oh my Lord
why do I cry?

Oh my Lord
why do I want to die?

Oh my Lord
why do I love that guy?

Oh my Lord
why did he lie?

Oh my Lord
why did he tell me good-bye?

Oh my Lord
I sure do love that awful guy?

Mack

Written, June 15th, 1975

My brother's a quack,
his name is mack.

He lives on a shack
the color is black.

He tried out for track
but couldn't get the nack.

He started to hack
now he'll never be back.

Flowers

Written, June 16th, 1975

I have some flower's,
that are pretty to me.

She said, they were pretty,
I said, how kind of thee.

They grow so high
cause of the bumble bee.

I would never sell them
so that everyone could see.

When I wake to my flower's
I am full of glee.

Mo

Written, July 5th, 1975

I know a man
his name is Mo.

He likes to play
tick tack on my toe.

When I say no
he shall surely feel low.

When I say blow
He will always go.

Cat's

Written, August 15th, 1975

Cat's are funny
they love to sleep.

When they wake,
they make no peep.

Cat's climb tree's,
with only one leap.

Cat's don't eat much,
Then back to sleep.

Work

Written, August 17th, 1975

I work all day
and never get done.

I work in a shop
and make gun after gun.

I work very hard
believe me it's no fun.

I work by myself
I work with no one.

When I got home
I rest in the sun.

The Beloved One

Written, August 18th, 1975

He came one day,
without a word.

He loved us all,
so that's what I heard.

Their were sick and injured,
they say what I heard.

He was the beloved one
he was no nerd.

He left one day and
returned on the third.

Where did he go, to
heaven i've heard.

Jack
Written, September 17th, 1975

I have a horse
his name is Jack.

I like to ride
upon his back.

I like to hear
the clickity clack.

Then one day he
Stepped on a tack.

Now I can never
Ride on his back.

I will never hear
Jack's clickity clack.

Billy Jack

Written, September 18th, 1975

They say he was an Indian,
his name was Billy Jack.

He lives upon a mountain,
in a small mud built shack.

The only time you saw him
is when someone's at your back.

No one gave him trouble,
or he'd make them his snake.

One day there was some trouble,
Or he'd make them his shack.

Three man came behind him,
but to all he gave a wack.

The woman all loved him,
They'd come to him in a pack.

The Bum

Written, October 10th, 1975

I know a bum
he's very dumb.

He drink's rum
From a big drum.

He eats a plum
he likes to chew gum.

He has a chum
that likes to chew gum.

He has a bad tum
thanks to his mum.

He lives in the slum
but isn't that dumb.

Love Me

Written, November 3rd, 1975

Why does life always
seem so blue?

Why is life so dull
please give me a clue.

With shoe's on your feet,
they're brand new.

With you by my side
some one not so true.

Please love me always
like I love you.

Heidi Renee

Written, November 3rd, 1975

We have a daughter
Her name's Heidi Renee.

She get's smarter and smarter,
with each passing day.

She's always so happy
and always so gay.

It makes me happy
to see her at play.

She's my little Heidi,
i'll teach her the way.

Tabitha Moss

The Pig

Written, November 5th, 1975

I know a man
he lives like a pig.

He fishes in ashtrays,
to find a cig.

He goes to the cupboard,
to eat old fig.

He's a thief and a liar,
he's now in the brig.

Ned

Written, November 24th, 1975

My friend is Ned
so that's what he said.

On top of his head
was a bunch of red.

He lays in his bed
and acts like his dead.

His car's full of lead,
he likes to lay tread.

He say's he's he's been fed
Someday he will wed.

Tabitha Moss

Joe
Written, November 25th, 1975

I have a cow
his name is Joe.

When he walks
he moves so slow.

I won't stand near
him cause he stepped on my toe.

When I blow my horn
he will always go.

That's my story
Of poor old Joe.

Bad Friend's

Written, February 7th, 1976

Sitting at home all alone
on this bright sunny day.

When all of the sudden there was
a knock at my door, I said come
in and be gay.

They spent the night and
stayed the whole next day.

They've done this before
I really must say.

I wish that they
would just go away.

When my husband got home
they had nothing to say.

As a matter of fact
we didn't even stay.

When we got back
they had gone away.

They will never come back
cause we want it that way.

Friend's

Written, February 9th, 1976

Friend's are weird,
In their own little way.

They come to visit
day after day.

They can cheer you up
when you are gray.

They can make you
sad when you are gay.

Then all of the sudden
the friendship begins to decay.

They get mean and nasty
with cruel thing to say.

They will never come back
And that's all I pray.

Eye's

Written, April 4th, 1976

Eye's are so pretty
so big and so bright.
When they're in love
they have a gay light.
When they are mad
they want to fight.
When there in heaven
they are out of sight.

Frank

Written, April 16th, 1976

There was a man
his name is Frank.

One dark lonely night
he robbed a bank.

He had a gun that
just carried a blank.

When they caught him
he said it was a prank.

They said that's tough
you're going in the tank.

My Dog

Written, May 10th, 1976

I have a dog
her name is Bunnie.

Sometimes she is
so very funny.

She likes it outside
when it is sunny.

I love my dog she.
is my hunny.

The Mountains

Written, June 21st, 1976

High in the mountains
with the beautiful snow.

The birds in the sky
seem to move so slow.

The wind is a kicking
it's starting to blow.

It's getting colder
I've a frost bitten toe.

I'll go inside where
The snow can't blow.

Poor OL Ed

Written, July 21st, 1976

There was a man
his name was Ed.
Down the street
you can see his shed.
He went to the doctor
and the doctor said,
Ed my good man
that will need some thread.
Then the doctor said
There now stay in bed.

Miscarriage

Written, August 20ᵗʰ, 1976

No one know's the horror
in a mother's eye's.

No one knows the pain
when her unborn child dies.

No one understands her
when she sit's and cries.

No one cares about her
no one even tries.

No one can feel the pain
when a mother's child dies.

No one knows the heartache,
when there's no answer to the why's.

The Bill

Written, August 27th, 1976

You go to the doctor
he tells you you're ill.

He writes out a paper
and says take a pill.

Then the next thing you
know you receive a bill.

Then suddenly your
better oh what a thrill.

Whoops not so fast
remember that bill.

I

Written, October 1st, 1976

I heard a knock,
upon my door.

I grabbed my glock,
and fell to the floor.

I put on my sock
and wishes for more.

I locked the lock
I was sure poor.

I went to the dock,
boy what a bore.

I throw a rock,
The fish got sore.

I put on a smock
And that's all I wore.

Heartache

Written, January 27th, 1977

As I sit here all alone
and see how much my baby's grown.

It breaks my heart to have to say
that her daddy's gone away.

We'll be alone forever
her daddy's been so clever.

He left one night
on a long long flight
for us never to see again.

It hurt so much
cause there's nothing to clutch.

I hope the girl he left with
is happy as can be.

She broken my heart but whats
even worse she hurt my little Heidi.

Happiness shall be no more
Since her daddy shut the door.

Big Shot

Written, February 13th, 1977

He thought he was a big shot,
he thought he was pro,

He thought he had a Robin,
but he only had a Crow.

He thought he had a reindeer,
but he only had a Doe.

He thought he was a tailor,
But he couldn't even sew.

He thought it would be sunny,
but it ended up just snowing.

He thought he had money,
but to every one did he owe.

Read-It

Written, February 21st, 1977

If you're walking down the street
and see something you like buy-it.

If you go into a restaurant and
see something new try-it.

If you're walking in the mall and
See a crowd be careful it could be a riot.

If you walk into the library
You'll see a sign that says quit.

If you like fattening food
don't remember your diet.

If you own a big plane
Remember fly-it.

My Daughter

Written, February 22nd, 1977

I have a little daughter
she's happy as can be.

I love to watch her in the sun
she's so full of glee.

It fills my heart with
happiness, to see her run so free.

To everything i ask of her
She'll never disagree.

She gets so unhappy
When she falls and skins her knee.

She'll always be my daughter
Because she's part of me.

The Little Man

Written, February 24th, 1977

Up upon a hill there
is a little house.

There's a man up there
that lives with his wife.

This man is so unhappy
his wife is such a louse.

He gets so lonley sometimes
he talks to his friend the mouse.

All Alone

Written, June 15th, 1977

Here I sit all alone
feeling oh so blue.

Knowing that my love is gone
there's nothing I can do.

While sitting here praying
that his love for me grew.

For I told him that I loved him
and to him i'll always be true.

When Thing Are Grey

Written, November 5th 1977

All around when
things seem gray,

and it feels like
it's a hell of a day.

Just remember this
thing I say:

Look at the bird
so high in the sky.

Look at the child
with the tears in his eyes.

But most of all look at the
children and don't make them cry.

Tabitha

Written, March 3rd, 1978

I have another daughter
Tabitha is her name.

I'll always keep her picture
in a little gold frame.

The day was november 29th,
on which she finally came.

My heart shall always burn for her
like that of a candle's flame.

So Hard

Written, March 16th, 1978

Why is it so hard
to touch a real dove?

Why is it so hard
to see true god above?

But most of all;
why is it so hard
to express true love?

House on The Hill

Written, September 29th, 1987

There once was a house
way up on a hill.

When the wind blows in
you can feel the chill

Out in the backyard
sita a bar-b-que grill

Why out in the field
it's a non-working drill

The people that lived there
became just a little ill

If they hadn't gotten well
They'd live there still.

Mommy

Written, February 4th, 1988

Mommy, mommy
if you only knew!

How much I loved you
truly I do!

The only thing better
that I can see!

Is how much you
could truly love me!

Yesterday; Today

Written, December 12th, 1989

Yesterday I was just a little girl
today I am a woman.

Yesterday was dolls and thing
Today is just one man.

Yesterday was games and such
Today is cleaning house and kids.

Yesterday was just the start
Today is the rest of my life.

Ernie

Written, June 27th, 1999

He has brown eyes
and matching hair.

With skin so brown
and a heart that fair.

I love you now
i'll love you forever.

I trust and believe in you
I shall leave you never.

You've healed my heart
my mind, body and soul.

I now give them all to you
with one final goal.

I want you to love me
till the very end we will be.

From

Written, June 28th, 1999

From the touch of your hands
to the kiss from your lips
from the cares of your tongue
to the thrust of your hips.
I couldn't desire you more.

From the beauty of your smile
to the warmth of your eye's
from the beat of your heart
to the sound of your sight.
I couldn't want you more.

From the bottom of my heart
to the depths of my soul
from the whole of my body
to the mind that you stole.
I couldn't need you more.

From all that is right
to all that is wrong
I will love you forever
You're my whole life long.
I couldn't love you more.

Tear

Written, July 4, 1999

Within my heart
lives a single tear
as I cry each night
when you're not near.

Within my mind
lives hope and joy
that you don't play with me
like a child with a new toy.

Within my soul
lives love and happiness
treat it gently
and we will live in bliss.

With all I have
I give to you
my heart, my love, my very soul
Remember this in all you do.

I love you babe
and I give to you
my very life
to care for it.

Touch

Written, July 5th, 1999

You've touched me with your eyes
You've touched me with your voice
You've touched me with your hands
In which i truly rejoice.

You've touched me with your body
You've touched me with your mind
You've touched me with your lips
In which you are one of a kind.

Please touch me with your heart
Please touch me with your soul
Please let us write as one
In which you'll make us whole.

Thank You

Written, August 18th, 1999

Thank you my love
you sharing your life
with me.

Thank you my love
for allowing me to share
my life with you.

Thanks you my love
For loving me so completely.

Thanks you my love
You all that happiness and joy
That you have brought
Into my world.
I love you

Our Love

Written, August 19th, 1999

As we walk along hand in hand
Through life's open door
Never wondering what we've missed
You always looking for more.

Through good and bad
i'll stay beside.
Whether happy or sad
i'll always love you.

Fate put us together
and forever and ever
I will always be true to you.
No matter where you are
No matter what you do
I truly truly, love you

Rain

Written, August 19th, 1999

The rain falling down
like the tears of my soul
like the loss of an old love
like the fear of a new.

The hail beating the window panes
like the beating of my heart
like the loss of and old touch
like the thrill of a new.

The snow floating gently to the ground
like the thought of my mind
like the loss of old memories
like the joy of making new.

The rainbow reaching end to end
like the love I have to give
like the loss of an old love
like the beginning if a new.

Wolf's Cry

Written, June 15th, 2007

The whisper of the wind
water trickling close by.

From high on the hilltop
is a lonely wolf's cry.

The moon shining brightly
the star's twinkling up high.

Still high on the hilltop
a lonely wolf's cry.

Way in the distance
is another wolf's cry.

As they come together
on the hilltop way up high.

Not one but two
now there's more.

As they sing to the moon
They are lonely no more.

Friends

Written, November 10th, 2005

I am your friend
tried and true
I spend my time
Commenting and messaging you.

Form the break of dawn
to the middle of the night
I write to my friends
and is feels so right.

From page to page
I am running around,
to my old or new friends.
With hug I am bound.

So be my friend
tried and true
and always remember
I am sending you love.

Music Of The Night

Written, July 30th, 2007

The sound of the night
are a wonderful delight
sitting here in my chair
by the flickering firelight.

Listing to the falling rain
as it taps gently on the window frame.

Hearing the hoots of an owl
in the distance a lone wolf howl.

The whisper of the trees
as they sway in the breeze.

The music of the night
till dawn comes the light
it's magic you see
as god watches over you and me.

Tabitha Moss

Love
Written, On An Unknown Date

Love should be tender
Love should be kind
Love should be forever
Love is a special find.

You've used my body
You've played with my mind
You've never really loved me
You've left my heart behind.

You've told me you're story
I've told you part of mine
I've loved you from the start
For your love I still fine.

So love me tender
don't close your heart door
For i shall love you forever
and never ask you for more.

Family

Written, January 28th, 2012

The whisper of the wind
the silence of the night
Watching but the window
With a moon that's bright.

The branches swaying slowly
A slight chill is in the air
As winter creeps upon us
With lots of love to share.

Families gather round about
Memories to through
Some that bring us happy thoughts
And some just makes us blue.

The silence of a falling tear
Rolling slowly down a creek
The sadness that is felt so strong
As memories of the mind speaks.

A warm and caring family
Can heal a heart that broke
Hugs and understanding
and loving words are spoken.

Printed in the United States
By Bookmasters